First, I want to say thank you for purchasing this book. I made this activity book during a global pandemic where things are very uncertain and scary. It feels like the entire world was put on pause, but life continued to happen. You still have to do all the adult things with limited resources. You kind of have to make a way out of no way right now. This time has given a lot of us a moment to sit and reflect on the decisions we've made in life, the people we hold near and dear to us, and what we see for our own futures.

For me, I was so content being the person that I was that I didn't see the way that I was constantly being my biggest enemy. The things I held on to from my past that hurt me were stopping me from building a better life for myself. The insecurities and pain I felt from previous heartbreaks were being carried into the next relationship. I was allowing friends to treat me any way out of fear of losing them. Because I had felt the pain of losing someone before, I didn't want to feel it again. That fear was causing me to miss out on life. I would say "never again" and I thought I really meant that, but it's easier said than done.

I had to learn that nobody is going to want for me more than me and I had to get back to doing things for me. Whether it was saying "yes" to that date that maybe wasn't my type or leaving the job that made me the most comfortable, stepping out on faith was the best thing I could've done for myself. You can't let fear and the past stop you from living life and taking a chance on yourself. My favorite quote is from one of my favorite childhood tv shows. The dad told his daughter "Sometimes life will knock you down. And that's okay. But what's not okay is letting life keep you down." It's okay to fail and mess up. It's okay to be scared and cautious. But faith is the exact opposite of fear. It's faith that drives you to be better and do better. It's faith that makes us what God called us to be. It's faith that leads to action. You have to have faith to know that you know what's best for you and better will come. You cannot change what you cannot control. We create our own happiness. The road to that happiness gets rough sometimes but that is no reason to stop. You have to keep living and keep praying and keep fighting. Even when things aren't going your way, you still have a purpose. So don't dwell on the negative. Focus on the little joys in life so you can find big joy in life.

I dedicate this book to all of the beautiful women in my family,

my best friend Carmen, my partner in crime Chelsie,

And to my heart and soul, my mother, Diane

God is love,

Self Reflection

Have you ever sat and thought about yourself? Your actions, your past, your personality? Self reflection is important. It is the key to self awareness, to look at yourself with interest and curiosity. Take a moment for self-reflection. What are some of the highs and lows from your life? How have they changed you? Do you have any "what-ifs"? What are some words of wisdom you'd give to you?

Go Get Your Man!

Sis, you are late for your date! Your man is waiting for you at the restaurant! Get to him!

Law of Attraction

The law of attraction is the ability to attract things that we focus on into our lives. The law of attraction uses the power of the mind to translate whatever is in our thoughts and make it a reality. Think about what you have attracted into your life. What is good? Think about what you would like to attract. Do these things serve you?

Things you have attracted into your life	Things you wish to attract into your life
______________________________	______________________________
______________________________	______________________________
______________________________	______________________________
______________________________	______________________________
______________________________	______________________________
______________________________	______________________________
______________________________	______________________________

I Said
what
I Said

Crossword

ROMANCE MOVIE EDITION

Down

2. 1997 movie about a photographer and a writer who fall in love in Chicago before the photographer decides to mend things with her ex

3. The college Monica and Quincy went to in 13-Across

4. Female star of 13-Across and 10-Down

6. What Stella was looking to get back in Jamaica

8. Rapper and actor who was the star of 12-Down

9. Book turned film about five couples whose relationships get tested by a book

10. 2002 romance movie about two friends who love hip-hop and each other

12. 1993 movie starring Janet Jackson, who uses poetry to ease her way through the difficult daily life in South Central Los Angeles

14. Dre Ellis, in 10-down

Across

1. What Lucky was driving in 12-Down

5. Comedian and television host who published 9-Down in 2009

7. The driving force of all romantic movies

11. Quincy McCall, in 13-Across

13. Romance movie released in 2000 about a couple whose love of basketball bring them together throughout the years

15. Author of the 1996 romance novel, How Stella Got Her Groove Back

16. Female lead in 2-Down

17. Dre's love interest in the 2002 romance movie, Brown Sugar

18. Comedian and actor who starred in 9-Down

19. Star of the 1996 romance movie, How Stella Got Her Groove Back

Goal Digger

We love reaching our goals and setting new ones. What are your goals in these five areas?

● Spiritual

____

____

____

____

____

● Professional

____

____

____

____

____

● Physical

____

____

____

____

____

● Financial

____

____

____

____

● Relational

____

____

____

____

Life
Is
Beautiful

Guess The Song

Part 1

The emojis below make a song title when they're all put together. Can you guess them all?

1. _______________________________

2. _______________________________

3. _______________________________

4. _______________________________

5. _______________________________

6. _______________________________

7. _______________________________

8. _______________________________

9. _______________________________

10. _______________________________

Take a Selfie

We all have a responsibility to love ourselves, inside and out. When you truly love yourself,
you have power and confidence in your skills, abilities, and emotions.

What is your favorite thing about yourself?

____

____

Why are you worth knowing?

____

____

What do you want the world to know
about you?

____

____

If you could make your life into a movie, what
would it be called?

____

____

Would you date you?

____

____

Sudoku

				8				9
	2			6	1	3		
			7		4		8	6
							1	
	1	6			2			
4		2			5			
		5	1			9	3	
			2	9		5		8
					7		4	

Hard Truth

We all go through things in life that teach us lessons and sometimes, the lesson is something you never expected. There are lots of simple truths in life that we have to accept like death is imminent or the perfect partner doesn't exist. But there are other truths that we learn about as we experience and go through life. What is the hardest truth you've had to learn?

Find your bae and circle his name, then find the
rest of ours!

L R M B B I T W P S X J D Z O D
S U O M I C H A E L E A L Y L A
D E R E K L U K E U Z M D R E M
B G R O Y C D I T F O I Y L O S
A C I E L E E D A U G E H A B O
S Z S G U P C R Y W K F A R I N
D D C G K F M I E O Q O O E R I
E H H S E X R S D P O X W N I D
T G E B J I A E I S P X D Z S R
D W S J A Y T L G T F E F T I I
C R T R M D E B G E E F J A F S
D E N Z E L W A S H I N G T O N
A J U S S E E R P V S D P E K E
P U T D R A K E I H U V T P Y T

Morris Chestnut
Larenz Tate
Luke James
Damson Idris

Idris Elba
Denzel Washington
Derek Luke
Jamie Foxx

Drake
Kofi Siriboe
Taye Diggs
Michael Ealy

Self Care

One of my favorite things to do is self care. Taking long baths, getting massages, and taking day trips alone are my favorite ways to rejuvenate my mind and reset my life. What are your favorite ways to spoil yourself? Do you buy yourself gifts? What are the things you would like to attract into your life to bring you peace?

Self Care Things

♥Things That Make Me Happy

Affirmations

Dont Worry
Be Yoncé

Let's flex that noggin. All of the first names in this quiz are six letters long and are hidden in two or more words of the clue sentence. Each sentence has a hint as to the gender most often associated with the name. I'll help you with the first one.

1. There's danger, Al. Don't lead your men that way.

Gerald

2. When you finish writing your feminist blog, lend a hand with dinner please.

3. Be truthful with him, or risk losing his trust.

4. Don't grab, rend, and rip her dress!

5. Hiking and camping are the boy's favorite things.

6. After she broke her femur, I elevated her spirits with my jokes.

7. The men waged war during farming's off-season.

8. "My garden is easily my favorite place," said the girl.

Write a love letter to yourself. No for real, you deserve it. Use this as a pick-me-up when you're down.

If you wish to move mountains
tomorrow, you must start by
lifting stones today
- African Proverb

Love Maze

Love is a maze sometimes. Find your way to the end.

Let's Dig Deep

What keeps you smiling on the worst of days?

____

____

____

____

____

What do you think is the best part of life?

____

____

____

____

____

FLOWER
CHILD
BEAUTIFUL
CHILD

You know the deal, guess the phrase or word based on the clue in each box.

TO CH U	S S S S B B B B A A A A R R R R G G G G	MAN ——— BOARD
T H WE'VE GOT E M	STANDING **MISS**	**VAD ERS**
ǝlddɐǝuᴉd **Cake**	JOBINJOB	GIVE GET GIVE GET GIVE GET GIVE GET

1. _______________ 2. _______________ 3. _______________

4. _______________ 5. _______________ 6. _______________

7. _______________ 8. _______________ 9. _______________

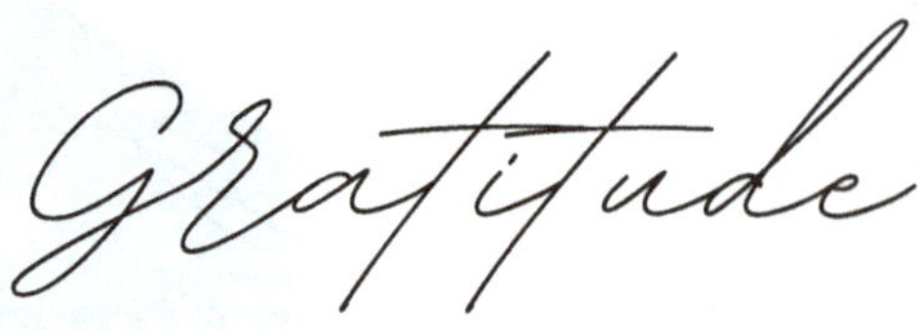

Gratitude

Take a moment to think about all of things you are grateful for. Write them down and release the positivity into the universe.

What I Am Grateful For

____

____

____

____

Lessons I'm Grateful For Learning

____

____

____

____

Things I Do To Remain Thankful

____

____

____

____

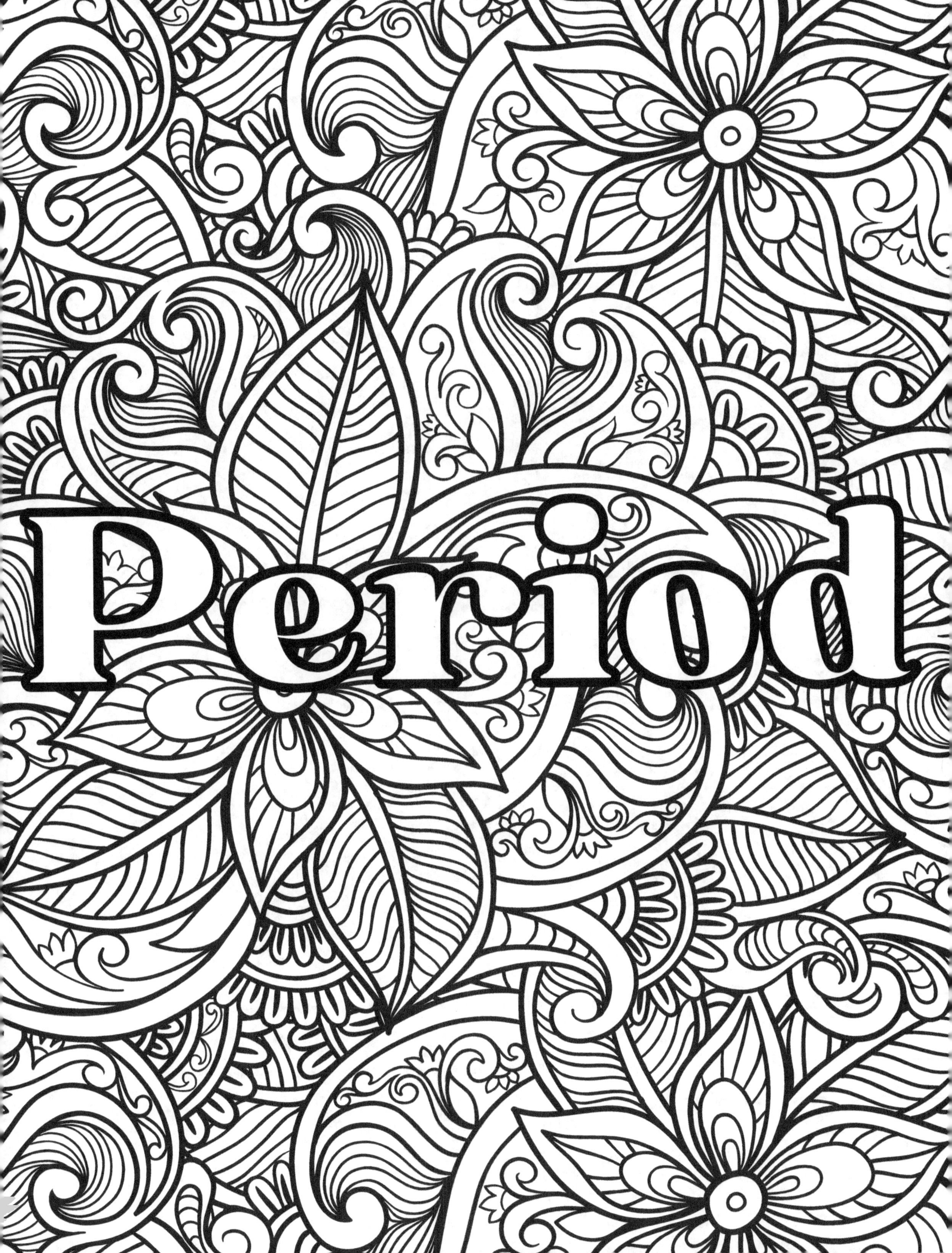

Period

Brain Teaser

These questions should make you think. But don't think too hard, the answer may be easier than you think!

Turn me on my side and I am everything. Cut me in half and I am nothing. What am I?

___

I am heavy and hard to pick up, but backwards I am not. What am I?

___

What can be seen once in a minute, twice in a moment, and never in a thousand years?

___

If you have me, you want to share me. If you share me, you don't have me. What am I?

___

What five-letter word becomes shorter when you add two letters to it?

___

Soundtrack

What is the soundtrack to your life? If you could pick three songs to best describe you, what would they be and why?

Track 1. _______________________________________

____

____

____

Track 2._______________________________________

____

____

Track 3._______________________________________

____

____

____

We Outside

Your bestie put you on the guestlist for the club tonight but you have to find your way there! Remember, it's free before 11 and it's already 10:45!

Forgiveness

We've all been hurt by someone. Use this space to process your feelings. This person may never see this letter but it'll be good for you to heal and let go.

Our hair, our way. Find the hairstyles in the word search below.

```
Q E T Y G L P W C H S K D O B D
S M R B P D A E T X E P V Y O A
K E T O C L U A E U A M D R B M
K I R H B C D V T E S D U L I S
N C N E O L T E U N G B H S A A
O Z S K D A C R B R A I D S R F
T I C G Y C L N Z H Q R N E D R
L J H S W E U S V P I E X P Y O
E G E A A F A R I E P G D Z S R
S W F J V R K L L S W S H T X Z
S R T R E O E B G S E C J B F S
D E N P O N Y T A I L I L S U N
A G T E S T E Q P V S G W M K N
C H U D E E P W A V E Z T P E T
```

Afro	Curls	Knotless
Bob	Deep Wave	Lace Front
Body Wave	High Bun	Ponytail
Braids	Kinky	Weave

In the last journal prompt, we talked about forgiving others. In this one, we're going to let go of all of the past hurt, trauma, and experiences. It's time to move-on. Fill in the blanks and read them back to yourself. If you need to, read them back every day. Whatever it takes, sis.

Today, I am letting go of

__________________________. Although I was

____________ by this situation, I will not

allow ____________________ to shape who I

am as a person. I am better than

________________ and today is my last day

holding onto it. I am stronger than I know.

I am bigger and I am better. I learned from

this experience and I will not allow

____________________ to happen to

me again. I forgive myself for

__________________. I love myself for

being better. I let go of

____________________ and I am happy.

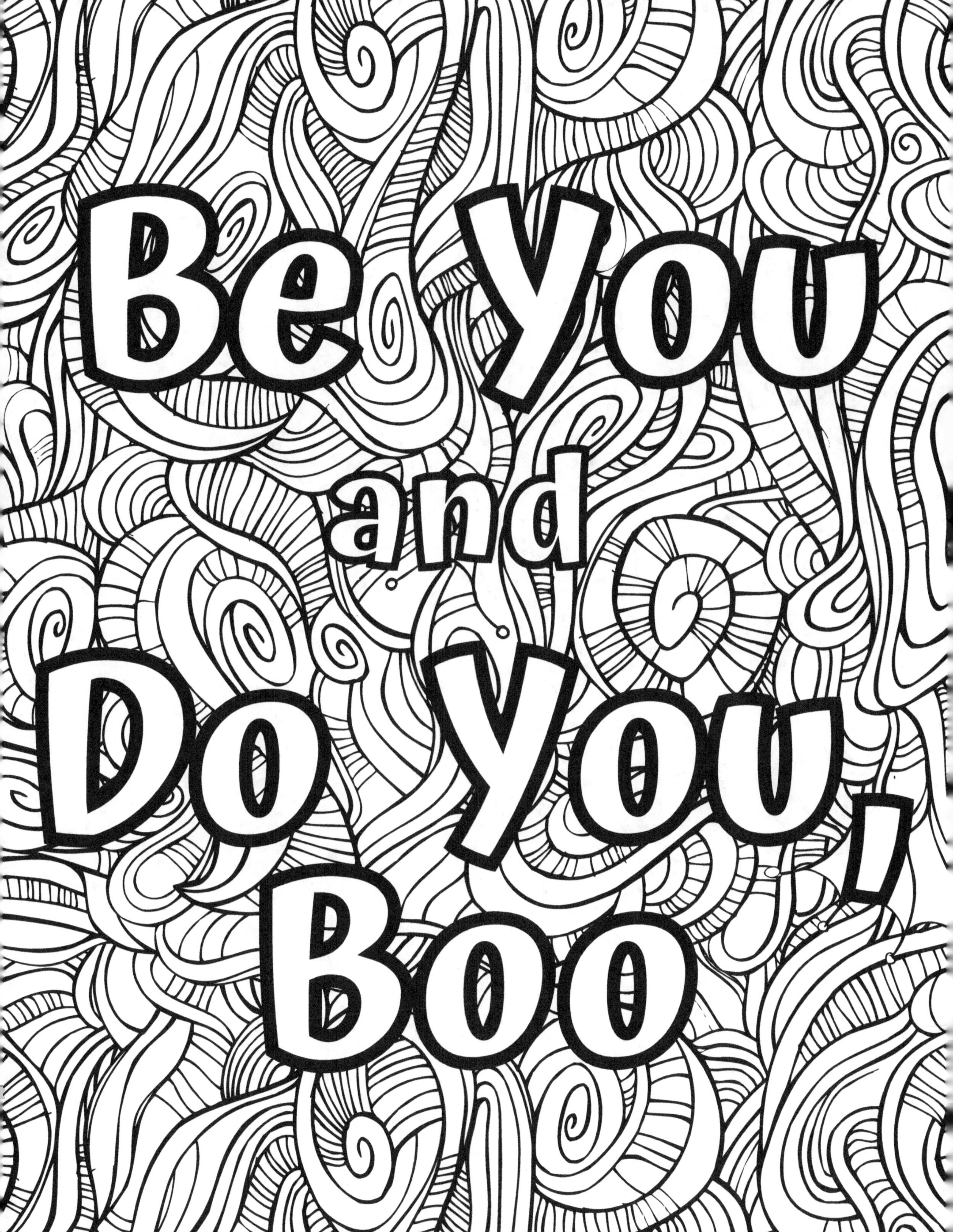

Be You
and
Do You,
Boo

Brain Game

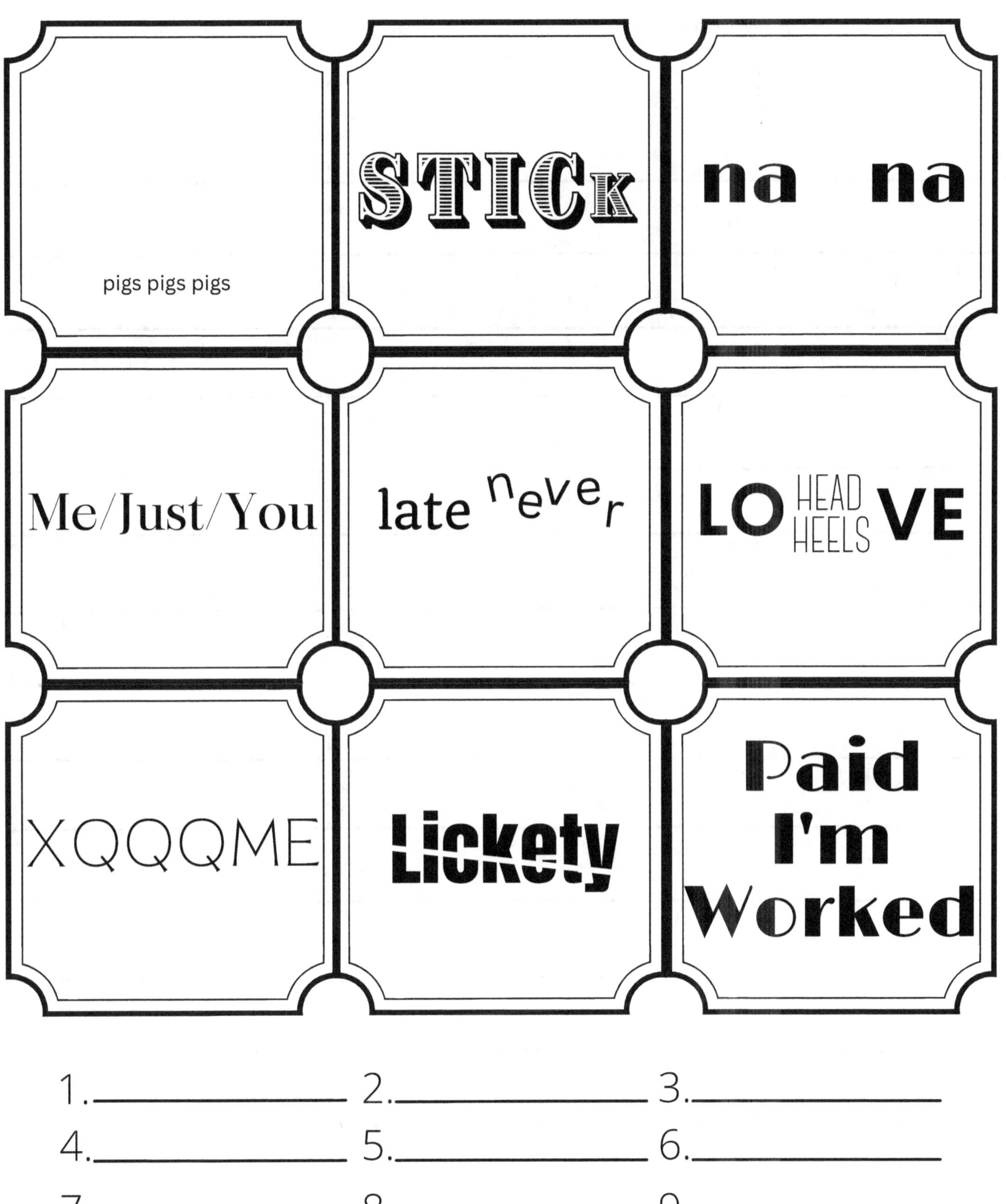

1.____________ 2.____________ 3.____________

4.____________ 5.____________ 6.____________

7.____________ 8.____________ 9.____________

And The Winner Is

Write yourself an acceptance speech for an award you will win one day (We're speaking, or writing, into existence.)

FIERCE

Get To The Bag!

Ooh girl! Telfar is having a sale! Make your way to the store for your new bag!

Self Love

There is no one in this world who will love you more than you. You should be your own biggest fan! Finish these statements about yourself and realize the greatness in you.

I am the greatest there is because

____

____

____

____

____

____

I am the the best version of myself because

____

____

____

____

____

____

Me
Myself
And I
A "BLACK GIRL MAGIC" FILM
QUEEN

Sudoku

			8			1		
7				1	2		6	
	3				9			
	5				7	8		6
		9		2		5	3	
8			6			9		
		6	4				1	
3				7	5			8

This one might be heavy so grab a tissue. Write a letter to your child self. Let them know about the lessons you've learned, where you're at in your life right now, what you want them to change on their journey, and how much you love them. This letter could help someone else, make it count.

Get Out Your Feelings

Brain Game

These are a little more difficult, good luck.

3.to
4.blame

moonce**on**

l l
e e
g g
g g
g g
g g
s s

JOB

Funny Words
Funny Words
Words
Words

b   e   d

No   No
———————
Right

noonT

Please

1.___________ 2.___________ 3.___________
4.___________ 5.___________ 6.___________
7.___________ 8.___________ 9.___________

It's Just Emotions Taking Me Over...

One thing we all dread talking about is our emotions. Our emotions tend to get us in trouble if they aren't clearly communicated. Here are a few questions to help you tap into your emotions today.

Make a list of all your emotions right now – what comes to mind first?

____

____

What is your unique emotional strength?

____

____

What emotions are you attached to?

____

____

What brings you joy?

____

____

In your opinion, are you emotionally stable? Why, or why not?

____

____

Keep
It
Lit

Here we go again! Don't think too hard!

What has a head, a tail, is brown, and has no legs?

____

What 11 letter English word is always pronounced incorrectly?

____

What can be measured but has no length, width, or height?

____

What can travel around the world while staying in a corner?

____

What fruit is always sad?

____

In This Moment

What do you need? By that, I mean what do you need right now in this moment to make you feel grounded and happy? Is it love, a real friend, a better mindset? If you could ask God for anything and it would appear right now, what would you ask for and why?

Real Hot
Girl
Shit

Guess The Song

Part 2

These are a little more difficult. Some of the clues sound like the answer. Pay attention!

1. _______________________________

2. _______________________________

3. _______________________________

4. _______________________________

5. _______________________________

6. _______________________________

7. _______________________________

8. _______________________________

9. _______________________________

10. _______________________________

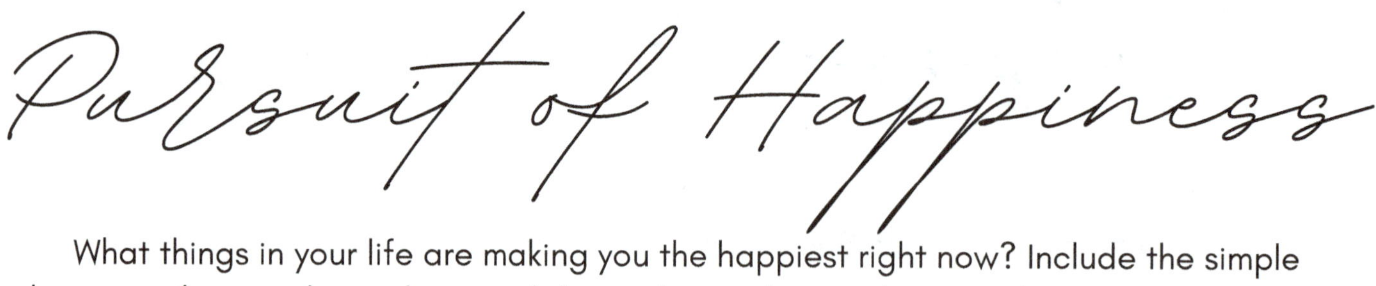

Pursuit of Happiness

What things in your life are making you the happiest right now? Include the simple pleasures, the people you love, and things that make your heart smile. How do you hold on to these things? Why do they make you happy?

It's
Giving
BOSS
BITCH

Crossword

STARS EDITION

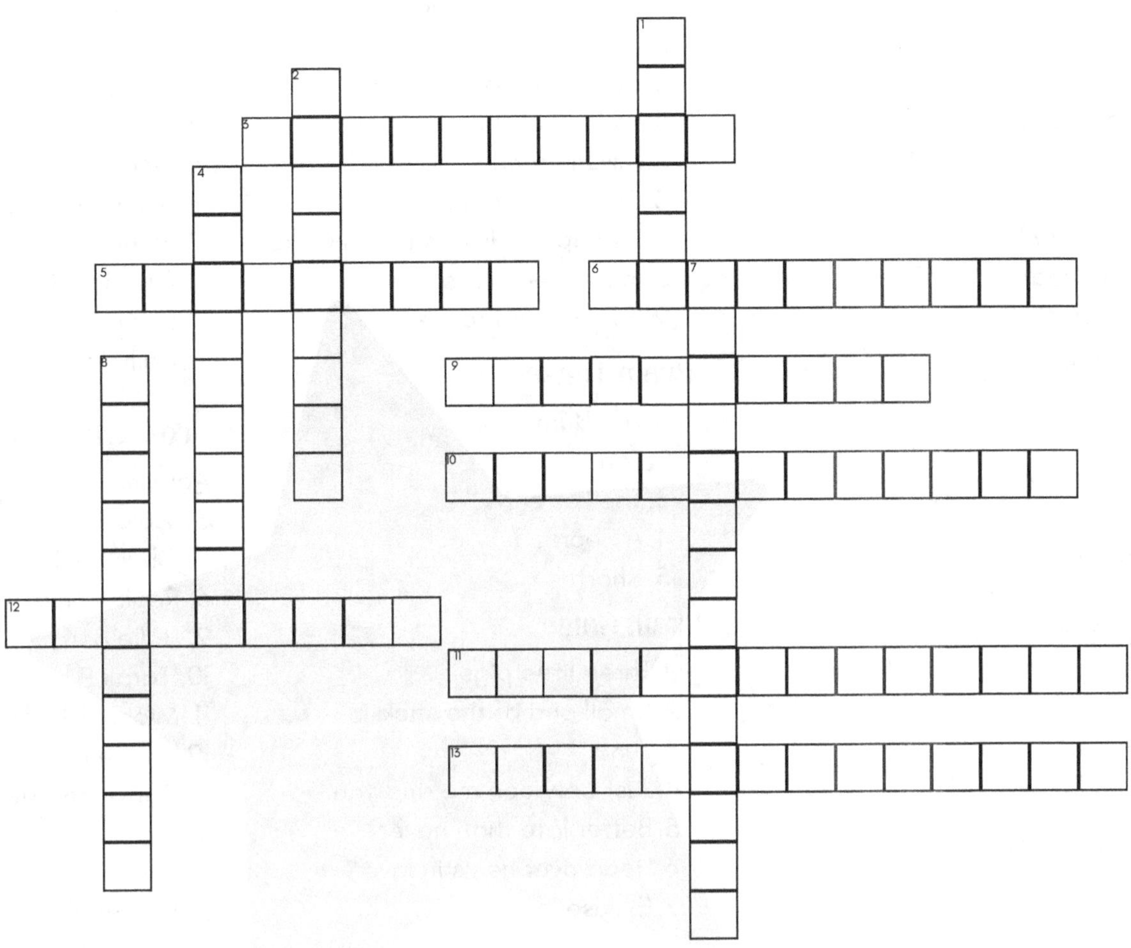

Across

3. Actor and producer who is the first African American to achieve the Triple Crown of Acting

5. Comedian and actor who got his start on SNL in 1990. He also released his first documentary, Good Hair, in 2009

6. Actress and director who starred in 227 as Brenda Jenkins

9. Actress whose breakout role was in the 1992 film, Boomerang. She was voted the most beautiful woman alive in 2008

10. Actress who was nominated for an Emmy Award for Outstanding Lead Actress in a Drama Series for her role as Cookie Lyon on Empire

11. Actor, singer, dancer, and entertainer who is hailed as the King of Pop

12. Singer, comedian, and actor who is known for his role in the biographical film, Ray. He also had a television show named after him

13. Actor who was nominated for an Academy Award for Best Actor for his role in Hustle & Flow

Down

1. The Artist Formerly Known As...

2. Actor that is known for his big personality, which he displayed in his classic 90's sitcom, The Fresh Prince of Bel-Air

4. Actor best known for his roles in Love Jones and Why Do Fools Fall In Love

7. Actress who breakout role was in the 2000 hit film Bring It On

8. Comedian and actor that is praised as being the reason SNL stayed on the air, he also won a Golden Globe for his role in Dreamgirls

Answer Key

Crossword Romance Movie Edition

Down
2. Love Jones
3. USC
4. Sanaa Lathan
6. Groove
8. Tupac
9. Think Like A Man
10. Brown Sugar
12. Poetic Justice
14. Taye Diggs

Across
1. Mail truck
5. Steve Harvey
7. Love
11. Omar Epps
13. Love And Basketball
15. Terry McMillan
16. Nia Long
17. Sidney
18. Kevin Hart
19. Angela Bassett

Guess the Song (Part 1)

1. California Love
2. Dear Mama
3. Thong Song
4. Rock with You
5. Off the Wall
6. Angel of Mine
7. No Scrubs
8. End of the Road
9. Brown Sugar
10. Lighters Up

Name Game

1. Gerald
2. Glenda
3. Morris
4. Brenda
5. Gareth
6. Muriel
7. Edward
8. Denise

Brain Game

1. You're out of touch
2. Up for grabs
3. Man over board
4. We've got them cornered
5. Misunderstanding
6. Space invaders
7. Pineapple Upside Down Cake
8. In between jobs
9. Forgive and forget

Brain Teaser

1. The Number 8
2. Ton
3. The Letter M
4. A Secret
5. Short

Brain Game

1. Three little pigs
2. Small end of the stick
3. Tuna
4. Just between me and you
5. Better late than never
6. Head over heels in love
7. Excuse me
8. Lickety split
9. I'm under paid and over worked

Brain Game

1. No one to blame
2. Once in a blue moon
3. Long legs
4. Inside job
5. Too funny for words
6. Bedspread
7. Right under the nose
8. Afternoon tea
9. Pretty please

Brain Teaser

1. A Penny
2. Incorrectly
3. Temperature
4. A Stamp
5. A Blueberry

Guess The Song (Part 2)

1. Empire State of Mind
2. Gangsta's Paradise
3. Stronger
4. Remember The Time
5. Who Can I Run To?
6. Bump Bump Bump
7. Bleeding Love
8. Birthday Song
9. Pony
10. Hail Mary

Crossword Stars Edition

Across
3. Viola Davis
5. Chris Rock
6. Regina King
9. Halle Berry
10. Taraji P Henson
11. Michael Jackson
12. Jamie Foxx
13. Terrance Howard

Down
1. Prince
2. Will Smith
4. Larenz Tate
7. Gabrielle Union
8. Eddie Murphy